MY MOTHER'S KEEPER

FINDING STRENGTH WITHIN THE BOND

MELANIE D. PHILLIPS

Destiny Discovered
Publishing, LLC

My Mother's Keeper
Published by Destiny Discovered Publishing, LLC
Copyright © 2021

This book is dedicated to the millions of mothers and daughters whose bond has been interrupted due to different challenges and/or struggles during these troubled times of the pandemic. The mother/daughter relationship can be very difficult at times but know that we stand in solidarity in support of one another. So, just know that your bond may be bruised or ruptured, but it is not broken. It can be repaired!

Table of Contents

Foreword

Someone once said, "A mother's love will never end; it is there from the beginning to the end," and can't we all agree? A mother sacrifices, leaving behind their personal wants and needs to ensure that their children have EVERYTHING they need. She gives unconditional love. She has both patience and understanding, and she will protect her children with the price of her own life!

As I reflect, I was blessed to have an amazing mother who displayed these characteristics to her children and grandchildren. I was in awe of her selflessness and enamored with her heart that was big enough to give each of her family members equal parts. I was able to transfer those characteristics and skills when I mothered a family of my own.

In her latest project, *My Mother's Keeper: Finding Strength Within the Bond,* Melanie D. Phillips introduces us to a special group who shares their experiences of being both child and parent. This anthology allows readers to look through their eyes and see the correlation between the relationships with their mothers and/or the relationships they had with their own children. I applaud the transparency and ability to keep readers engaged that these authors display and the phenomenal way that both lessons and healing are woven throughout the pages. Each story will not only encourage and inspire you, but it will cause you to reflect on and relate to all that she shares.

The Bible speaks of many mothers; some of those include Sarah, the mother who waited; Hagar, the mother who endured; Rebeka, the mother who believed; and Elizabeth, the mother who believed in miracles. These stories and reflections allow us to see the spirit of each of those women embodied through the legacy of her mother.

Thank you, Melanie, for sharing your gift of writing and encouraging others to tell their stories with the world.

Pastor Patricia Burt
Greater New Birth Church
Milwaukee, Wisconsin

No Longer a Dream, It Was Reality

By
Cheria Hollowell-Rush

"If you educate a man, you educate an individual,
but if you educate a woman, you educate
a whole nation (family)."

Dr. James Emman Kwegyir Aggrey

An educated girl becomes an educated woman. Her parent(s) instill the importance of education, family life, work life, and a spiritual life. Well, that is what my parents did, and I saw it firsthand in how my parents raised me and my siblings. Here, I will talk about the spiritual and family life aspects. There's no perfect family, but my family was perfect for me although, of course, we went through our shares of ups and downs like most families. I saw my parents work on the family, they played and hung out with us as a family, and we prayed together as a family. But I also witnessed how having a relationship with God helped increased their faith while dealing with certain situations, especially my mom. I remember it like yesterday when my mom, my little brother, and I were flying back home from Atlanta, GA, to Minnesota, and our takeoff was very turbulent. People gasped around us, and the flight attendants moved at a fast pace up and down the aisle as if they were not sure what was next to come. Which made me and little brother look at my mom to see if she seemed concerned.

I now know the meaning of a real poker face! My mom showed no expression at all. She might have been scared or anxious, but we wouldn't have ever known. Her body language and face were neutral. Meanwhile, the turbulence was so bad that my brother leaned over to our mom and asked, "Mom, are we going to make it? Will we be, ok?" My mom, sitting in the middle seat with me on one side and my brother on the other, said, "Give me a second, and let me ask God." She said that so fast as if she was waiting to pray without alarming us. My mom closed her eyes and grabbed both of our hands and began to pray silently, and within a second or two, she responded, "Yes, we will be ok." As my little brother laid his head on my mom's shoulder, and I held her hand, we both felt relieved. Needless to say, minutes later, the turbulence stopped, and my mom then voiced her opinion, "The air traffic controllers and/or the pilot should have known better to take off in such stormy weather!" I didn't say a word, but my thoughts were...EXACTLY!

For years, I thought my mother was my best friend. She started saying that to me as young as I could remember, and I played right into her hands. I told my mom practically everything, and she would use those conversations as learning tools. She would say, "These are the things you do; these are things you shouldn't do, and these are the things you better not do." What followed behind each conversation would be the reasoning why and the consequences. Those consequences were never anything that I wanted to deal with, especially at that age. I soon realized at the age of 13, however, that my mom was not my best friend when I told her something that one of my friends did, and she said, "I'm calling her mom!" My response was, "You can't do that. I thought you were my best friend!"

My mother answered forcefully, "I am, but I'm your mother first! If something like that occurred with you, and my friends knew and didn't share with me, then they would no longer be my friends. Unless they reprimanded you first. But not to do or say anything is absurd." My mom took it to heart when she often repeated that old African proverb "It takes a village to raise a child." Therefore, I knew my mom was going to call and tell her friend, and eventually, my friend and I grew apart.

Although growing up in church was very pivotal to my parents, I didn't really realize how having an intimate relationship with God was crucial until I got married. I was tested and tried in more ways than one. Yet, the tests that my husband and I endured in our marriage was solvable compared to what my mom was about to go through. One night when I was asleep, God showed me my mom and my dad drifting apart. I didn't see their faces, but I knew it was them. I woke up frantic, telling my husband what God revealed to me and then calling my best friend to share with her; neither of them believed it. They didn't dispute the dream, but they didn't believe it either. My best friends' words were, "The devil also can come to you in a dream as well." I knew God was one that could not lie, and I was praying that the dream wasn't real. In the next dream I had, God reassured me that it was He that was preparing me for what was next to come. Well, the dream came true, and that was the beginning of the end of their marriage. There were many tests my mom and I both endured separately and together. In some cases, it was like role reversal. I passed some of those tests while failing some, too. But God!

Dear Mom,

It's not often that I thank you for scolding me when I was a child, punishing me when I was a teenager after I snuck out the house, and giving me a stern tongue lashing after I started to ruin my credit as a college student; but I definitely remember those difficult moments, and now, I thank God for your discipline. I used to laugh and call you "Mommy Dearest" when I was younger, especially when you would make me clean up around the house, but now that I am an adult with my own family, I realize my home should always be presentable, and the presence of the Lord should be felt when anyone enters.

There are not enough words to describe how much I love you and appreciate everything that I've learned from you. You've shown me how to pray and cry out to God, helped me with struggling friendships, provided marital advice, encouraged me when I was struggling in college, cheered me on when I graduated from college, and helped me negotiate my salary! I am where I am today because of your reassurance and support.

Thank you, Mom, for being my biggest cheerleader. You have pushed me continuously to work hard, and when I wanted to give up, you uplifted me. I can never repay you for all of the sacrifices that you have made for me and my brothers. You are such an inspiration and make motherhood look effortless; you are the true definition of a Proverbs 31 woman, and I am happy to be your daughter and best friend.

Love,
Cheria Hollowell-Rush

Unintentionally Reversed Roles

By
Melanie D. Phillips

Yea, though I walk through the valley of the
shadow of death, I will fear no evil; For You *are* with me;
Your rod and Your staff, they comfort me.

-Psalm 23:4

I was entering the valley of the shadow of death, and though I didn't fear evil, I wasn't sure if I would die in the valley. My heart was so broken that I thought I was going into cardiac arrest. But God assured me that I would survive the place that I had never entered before. He said, "It may get dark and seem dangerous in the valley before you will see light. Nonetheless, My rod and My staff are with you, and I will never leave or forsake you...Peace Be Still." How could one be still while in the fight of their life? Also, how could one be still in unforeseen circumstances? I would soon be to shaken to pray and didn't know what my life would look like after death...the death of my marriage, that is.

It was the week before my daughter Cheria's birthday, and I promised to take her out for dinner when I arrived back in town. She and her husband, along with some of her friends, had planned to celebrate her big day in Vegas, and I wanted to enjoy her before she left. I made reservations at the restaurant of her choice so that I could show her a great time.

I didn't expect that while traveling my ex-husband, he would drop an unexpected bomb on me that would affect all of our lives in one way or another.

I was imploding and exploding, trying to hold it together until after my daughter and I would meet up. Knowing that it would be impossible because hurt was written all over my face while I wore an invisible mask. I prayed to God that she would enjoy her dinner and still have a wonderful time after the news I was about to deliver. I held it together until dinner was over, and we walked backed to our cars. It was an overcast 41-degree day, and it was just enough chill in the air to feel it in your bones. Apparently, the sun must have been on vacation because the clouds looked like they were never going away. Or maybe that was just my mood. The wind was calm, and although it wasn't raining on the outside, my insides were flooded with tears of pain. I was about to erupt. I found myself bypassing my car and getting into hers. I told her that her dad asked me for a divorce while out of town. That is when the dam burst and the tears came rushing through.

Shock appeared in my daughter's eyes, yet she was calm. Her beautiful brown eyes widened like a doe, and without moving a muscle in her face, she said, "Mom, God showed me you and dad growing apart in a dream." I thought to myself, *why didn't He show me*, but I realized he showed her so she could be there in support of me. Initially, I thought she would need consoling, yet the roles were reversed. I needed her more than she would know. Instead of being the mother, I treated her as if she were my friend. I told her more than I should have and would never advise anyone to divulge so much information to their children. Nevertheless, she was there for me and her brother, praying for us day and night. She would come over to pray before she went to work, after she left work, and called when she couldn't come over. She checked on us several times a day.

One particular time, she stepped in and assumed the responsibility that my ex-husband would soon forfeit. I remember like it was yesterday the note that my leasing agent slid under my door that read, "Due to the amount of rent that was not paid, you will have eight days to vacate the premises." We had just sold our home, and we had dual residence at the time because his job relocated us to Michigan, and we were living in Wisconsin. The only reason I was still in Wisconsin was to finish my master's degree, and we had just purchased a hair salon. He told me that he would only be in Michigan working for two years and then return to Wisconsin to help expand the hair business. Yet, I was getting ready to be homeless if I didn't pay the remainder of the rent that I had no clue *wasn't* paid.

I immediately called the leasing agent, and she said, "Per your husband, you will be paying the remainder of the balance." It would have been nice if I would've known, but I guess that wasn't in his plans. Thank God, I wasn't out of town, or I would have come back to no place to stay. I guess I could've have stayed in our business, but business and pleasure don't mix...nahhh, I'm just kidding! I can now look back, make jokes, and laugh at such foolishness!

However, my daughter took it upon herself to pay the remainder of the rent, and although I had the money and begged her not to, she insisted.

My daughter was so concerned for me and her brother that she neglected her own responsibilities. Needless to say, she was strong around me but was broken at home. She would not share her feelings with me but unleashed them on her husband. Our bond was interrupted because I needed her and thought it was selfish of her to say that she needed to spend more time at home. How selfish was I? As grown as I was, I knew she needed to spend more time with her husband, but I needed her time with me as well. I was broken and hurt. We know that hurt people hurt people, but in this case, I was unintentionally hurting and breaking up my daughter's household. Both households were falling apart until we both agreed that she needed to spend more time with her spouse. We all were in the valley living one day at a time, but we eventually commanded our struggle to surrender to us instead of surrendering to it. Two of my best friends had already stepped in to support, so they just stepped up. I then started to study, pray, fast, and rely on God more than ever because no one can relieve your pain and give you peace like He can... No One! God knows who to send and what to do in time of need. It's sad to say that the decisions that one makes can affect everyone around and not just family but also friends. It was a domino effect. We were dysfunction-ally functioning...if that makes sense until we found strength and peace in the midst of the storm. As I exited the valley, my daughter and I began to strengthen our bond, and God was at the forefront of our relationship.

One of the best and worst schools that I've ever been to is the school of life. Life will interrupt and challenge the closest bond that you may have with someone. Yet, if one doesn't give up, there will be lessons to learn along the way. You will have a valley experience where there will be suffering and discomfort that will weaken and try even the best relationships. However, the pain of it will and can strengthen your bond if you do the work, have faith, and trust God.

The Valley Experience

By
Melanie D. Phillips

It wasn't easy being in the valley. It wasn't easy losing touch with my soul.

It was hard watching myself almost spiral out of control.

My spiral consisted of me being hurt and angry at the same time, while wearing an invisible mask that sometimes was hard to find.

I eventually found it but couldn't wear it when I conversed with God.

God created me, so He knew me, but He warned me that being in the valley would be extremely hard. He also said it would be worth it, that everyone who needed me would see how He would pick me up, dust me off, and create in me a different heart that would eventually help save me.

Thank you, Lord, for giving me a voice; thank you, Lord, for giving me a choice to choose heaven instead of hell. Heaven was where I wanted to be, but hell was truly calling me, so I fought constantly for my soul. I held on to God, and I wouldn't let Him go. God presented me with the spirits of forgiveness, peace, and strength so that I wouldn't lose control.

Also, He granted me grace then; I gave grace to myself, which allowed me to spiritually grow. The growth allowed me and my daughter to resume our mother/daughter roles.

Dear Cheria,

Did I tell you? That the day that I laid eyes on you my life changed?

I promised myself that I would protect you for the rest of your life. And yes, I was overprotective as you say, but your safety was always my concern. But to be honest, it was God that gave me instructions on how to raise you. Although there were certain times I felt as if I didn't always assume the responsibilities, I did the best that I could do. I learned quickly by your older brother that children don't come with manuals. Thus, by the time I had you, prayer was second nature, and talking to God was first. Therefore, God became an important part of our lives, and I'm proud that you've mirrored what you saw by learning to have a relationship with Him.

My babygirl! This was the nickname I gave you, and now you are a new mom. Just know that I'm extremely proud of you and the awesome mom that I know you will be. When you think your best is not good enough, remember that you are not perfect. But your imperfections will teach you how to improve yourself and be a better mom than you were the month, the week, or the day before. A great mother is not one who is defined by what she knows, rather by what she is willing to learn. Which will determine who you really are and what you will become. I know that you will be a great mom because you were and are a great daughter. I Love You!

Yours Truly,
Your Best Friend & Mom
Melanie D. Phillips

We Are Still Standing: From Tragedy to Triumph

By

LaTambria Johnson

As women, we tend to push through and try to always make it better for the ones we love. After having children, it becomes all about nurturing and caring for them. So, what does a mother do when that main task is put in jeopardy? Well, that's what my daughters and I experienced in 2012 and 2013.

Early 2012, I found myself marrying the man I thought I would love forever. My oldest daughter, Amaiyah, was almost five years old at the time and was so excited to be one of my flower girls. My baby girl, Mariah, was three and was my little mini bride! Everything was going so well. The girls were as spoiled as ever, but not too much. In July of 2012, I began to feel very weird at work and decided to go to the urgent care just to get checked out. I sat there for about an hour with my husband, and after a urine test and blood work, the doctor came in and said, "Congratulations!" We were both confused. He then went on to tell me I was about three weeks pregnant. So yes, we were shocked, to say the least, but super excited! We made it home to the girls and told them the news, and they were so excited. They talked constantly about what gender they wanted the baby to be and what they were going to help me with to care for the baby.

I began my routine visits with my doctor, who made sure to watch me closely because of the preeclampsia and premature birth with my daughter, Mariah. Early on, everything was going well. Early September, though, I went to an appointment, and my blood pressure was extremely high. She did a sonogram and noticed a large tumor near the baby. She then ordered me to have a nurse to come to my home every Wednesday to give me progesterone shots, which could help reduce the risk of premature labor. She also sent me once a week to a OBGYN specialist. He followed the tumor and pregnancy also and gave me meds to control my blood pressure. Everything seemed to be working. I was still going to work every day, caring for the girls, and living life as if nothing had changed. The tumor, in fact, didn't seem to be growing, but the baby definitely was.

We made it to 19 weeks and finally got to see the gender of our little bundle of joy. I prayed for a boy, and just like that, God gave me my boy! We were all so excited and immediately began to think of names. We came to the agreement of Amari Aubre' Carter within a few days. For some reason, though, things would ultimately become difficult. We began to argue more and, even a few times, things would become physical. It was never done in front of the girls, thank God. But I knew it was not right. Finally, I was told by my doctor that it was time for me to go on light duty at work and relax more because my pressure started rising a little again, and they did not want to take any chances. Things eventually calmed down between us then. I prayed and prayed and asked God to keep me through the pregnancy.

Thanksgiving came and, while sitting at the house with family, everyone noticed how swollen I had become. My feet looked as though they were about to explode. I wasted no time getting in the days following to see my doctor. She quickly got me in to the specialist again. They both agreed that it was time for strict bedrest. So, on December 4, 2012, I worked my last day for a long while. My nurse showed up as usual that next day to give me my shot and check my blood pressure. She came in and first tried twice to check my pressure, and it would not read. So, instead she gave me the shot first and tried the pressure again following. It still didn't read. She asked me if I felt ok, and I told her yes, I felt normal. So, she tried one last time, and it read 200/210. She grabbed me up off the couch and told me we had to go to the hospital now. I asked if I could get dressed first, and she said there was no time. She drove me, and my husband followed. I immediately went into mama mode, stressing about who would get the girls from school and daycare and who could watch them if they kept me.

As soon as we made it to the ER, my doctor was there, and they rushed me straight back and started all the monitors. My pressure had not decreased at all. They started me on IV meds to try to get it down, and magnesium to keep me from having a seizure. Still, I was asking for my phone to try to get things situated for the girls. All I could think of was them. Before my husband, it was just me and them, and they needed me. No one could do what I could. Finally, they took everything from me and told me I had to relax and, after my pressure was down, they would let me call whomever I needed to. They finally let my husband in the room with me, but I was so in and out and burning up because of the magnesium that I didn't remember much. Finally, my pressure went down. Amari was seemingly doing okay, and they let me call and setup what I needed to for the girls. My husband picked them up and got their bags together to go stay the night—I thought—with my sister.

The next morning, I was awakened by my doctor telling me that they were preparing the ambulance to transport me to another hospital with a better NICU for babies. So, my husband called and let everyone know I would not be coming home and what was going on. My family and friends rallied together to meet the needs of the girls and kept them blind to it all until I said otherwise. Still, I thought, "But what if they need something only, I can do? What if with them being so young they thought I just left them and forgot them?" When I made it to the next hospital and got situated, my mom and sister and a few other family members and friends came by to sit with me and try to make me comfortable. I asked if someone could bring the girls by after school, and my brother, who was in town from the Navy, did just that. When the girls arrived, I had them come to my bedside and told them I would be okay, and Amari would, too, and I would be home to them soon. They walked back over by my brother, and I saw my oldest break down into tears. I didn't know if she understood enough or what she felt, but I could not watch that. I asked them to take girls out and not bring them back in to see me like I was.

That evening, the specialist came in and told me he would be taking over for my doctor going forward until everything was back to normal. He explained to me that I was given two options: to fight a little longer and take shots that would help my son's lungs mature faster or let them take him right then. Well, I'm sure you knew my response. I fought and prayed and cried and endured so much. It got so bad that they could not find any more veins to use for my IV lines and had to start one in the only vein left: in my neck. Then December 8, 2012, came. Three days in the hospital, and my mom was sitting there with me. I was asking about the girls and then I told her they had not brought me anything to eat and that I was hungry. So, when the nurse came in, we asked about it, and she told me things were taking a turn with my body, and they were having me fast for an early-morning emergency C-Section. I asked to see my girls one last time before all that. I was trying to stay smiling and make it seem as if I were okay and would be out soon. In all honesty, I wanted to see them again…just in case it was the last time.

The morning of December 9, 2012, my family surrounded my bed and prayed with me before being sent to the waiting room. They took me back, and I only remember a little because I was in and out. I remember one moment I heard them say there is the baby, and I felt the pressure of them taking him out. I heard a slight whimper and saw them rush him out to the NICU. Then I heard the doctor say there was a second tumor. They removed the one they knew of, but there was a problem with the other. It was attached to my abdominal wall. They called in a specialist for that, and he stated that he would be surprised if me and my son survived. He told them if they wanted to save me, they needed to wait and remove that tumor later and get me some units of blood because I had lost way too much. So, they closed me up and left the tumor.

I spent a couple days in a special care room (ICU) in labor and delivery after. I could not breathe on my own, my blood count kept falling too low, my blood pressure was still crazy and, because of it all, I could not see my son or the girls. I suddenly kicked into mama mode and started pushing myself with the breathing exercise and relaxing to get my pressure down, and praying that God would instill within me the strength to be able to go see my son. Finally, I did, and he was doing great. My little fighter, breathing over their machines and fighting on.

On December 11, 2012, they moved me to a regular room, where I got to see and spend a long time with my girls, and they told me I would get to be released soon. One of my nurses, in fact, came in and said how blessed she was every day stepping into my room with my gospel playing and watching me fight diligently to stay in good spirits. She also told me how sick I really was: I had developed HELLP syndrome, and my organs were shutting down. The doctors really did not think I would pull through. But God had other ideas. I was discharged December 13, and my girls were so happy, but so distant. They were afraid to touch me, thinking they would hurt me. I finally told my oldest to pull the tree out the closet and, although I could barely move, I helped and watched them put up the Christmas tree after only a few days of being home. I wanted to try to bring back a sense of normalcy.

I let them go with me every day to visit Amari. They could not go in the NICU, but they were simply happy to go with us, and I would take pictures and show them videos. Amari made it through a successful intestine surgery and, by Christmas, was gaining so much weight. His main doctor told me to get the nursery ready because she knew he would be going home. Sadly, however, things didn't work out that way. On January 26, 2013, while she was on a vacation for a few days, and he was under the care of another doctor, Amari had suddenly passed away. I was lost, crushed, just could not understand. Still, no one could really explain how or why it happened to this day. How do you explain this to a 4- and 5-year-old? It was the hardest thing to do and a pain I would wish on no one.

On February 1, 2013, we laid my son to rest, and a little more than a week later, I had to put on that fake smile to try to have a birthday dinner with family and friends, all the while still trying to be normal for the girls. I sensed at the time I was dealing with some depression and was not being as attentive as before all this occurred. About two weeks later, I was back in the hospital for what was supposed to be a same-day surgery to remove the second tumor. I ended up being in there for four days and had to learn to walk and talk without the usage of the oxygen tank again, and even bring a breathing apparatus home to continue to build my lungs back properly.

By July 2013, we were preparing to take a family trip to the beach, and out of nowhere my husband decided he wanted to leave and go back to his home state. From the moment I was home until June things seemed to be ok. Then, out of nowhere my husband began making statements about missing his friends and family back home in Louisiana constantly. However, I had no idea that he would leave. I did not fuss or argue. I simply got my sister and her children to take the trip with us, and when I returned, I filed for divorce. That was my reality check that it was just me and my girls again, and we were going to live life to the fullest. We got stronger into church again and began to get out and do things the more my strength built.

Since then, I have been determined to show them nothing but a strong woman and how they should strive for all the greatest in life. There were days I found them comforting me when I would have a moment, and even to this day, they still do. Going through all this together bonded us even stronger. Even though they were young, they have amazing strength and knowledge and continue to strive for greater today. I am beyond proud to be their mother and thank God for guiding us on a path to grow through the hurt and pain and, most of all, to stand for each other. Not every day is easy, yet we are still growing together, and we celebrate Amari every year as if he were here.

Dear Amaiyah and Mariah,

There are so many things I can say about you two. But to start, let me say I thank God for blessing me to be a mother to both of you angels. We have endured many things together, and I know without you two I would not have made it through it all. You two are my driving force. I've always promised that no matter what we face, you will always see a strong woman who strives to stack up every stone as a building block to move forward. It has been beyond an honor to watch you both grow so much. Your drive, tenacity, and eagerness to grow and advance are a joy to watch. Doing this book project with you two has been nothing short of amazing. Life has so much more for the both of you, and I personally can't wait to sit back and watch, support, and cheer you both on all the way. As we know, not every day will be easy, but remember to keep God first, and He will forever guide you through everything He brings you to. I love you both with every fiber of my being, and I will forever be right here to help along the way! It's only up to even greater from here! WE ARE DESTINED FOR GREATNESS BECAUSE GOD SAID SO!

Love,
Mom

Amaiyah Ross
(LaTambria Johnson)

I remember when I was five years old, and my mom went to her first ultrasound. She was so excited. The next thing I remember was her getting rushed to the hospital. The next time I saw my mama was in a hospital bed, extremely sick, and I was very scared, thinking I was going to lose her. I did not want to leave her side. She gave birth to my beloved little brother, Amari Carter, on December 9, 2012. I was in the hallway with family, waiting on the nurses to roll my brother by us. This was the only time I saw my little brother. About a month and a half later, my brother was pronounced dead. On February 1, 2013, he was buried. After that, we started to get back into church, which was a great thing for us because seeking God really helped us come back together as a family. The more we attended church and listened to gospel music, the easier it was to try to grieve. Doing things like shopping, playing games, and coloring also brought us together and got our minds off of that dreaded situation. Now, we have a strong and healthy relationship. We still visit Amari in the cemetery, and though it can be emotional at times, we are closer than we've ever been as a Christ-centered family—with God, our Helper, guiding us.

Dear Mama,

Truth be told, there aren't enough words in the dictionary to thoroughly sum up just how much of an immeasurable impact and influence you've had on my life. I've witnessed you endure and navigate through so much turmoil, seen you persevere and clear so many hurdles, observed you shed many tears, yet I've been blessed to have a lifetime front row seat to arguably the biggest victories of your life. For these reasons—surely, there are a slew of others—you are my superhero, my Shero, to put it more precisely. For the rest of my life, you are always the one whom I credit for inspiring me the most. You are the bravest person I know. You have lost a child, walked out on your job that, quite frankly, added little to no value to your life and, in adding to and enhancing your beautiful legacy, you've become destined to start your own business. While you have had your share of turbulent times and wilderness experiences, one thing that I find especially intriguing about you is that never do you take defeat lying down, all the while exercising your faith in ways unimaginable. With God, we as a family collectively fought and made it through life's toughest of obstacles. As always, Mama, I appreciate you. I adore you. I honor you. I thank God for you. And most of all, it is my prayer that God infuses within me the Light of the Holy Spirit to carrying on your beautiful and amazing legacy.

Yours Truly,
Amaiyah

You Act Just Like Your Mother!

By

Jennifer C. Rogers

There has been a struggle between mothers and their daughters for centuries. The alpha female battle has gone down in houses around America for centuries and still exists today. So, what is it really about? What is behind the battle? For me, I didn't understand what my mother was trying to accomplish with all her opinions and rules until I not only had my own daughters, but I also experienced life. Once I got over 35, I began to understand what all that was about. Your mom will always understand what your issues will be because she knows what demons chased her and plagued her thoughts, emotions, self-esteem, and self-worth. They all lived with her at one time.

Good or bad, what's in you comes from the DNA that was received from your parents while in the womb. What you are predisposition to do is already written inside you and it's up to you to refine it, rebuke, or repair it. Good mothers fight for their children. They are willing to go to the mat in defense of their children. Willing to eat last when food is limited, wear the same clothes when money is funny. Literally willing to sacrifice their very life just so you could live.

My mom died 14 years ago, and I wish I could tell her I finally understand. I understand the pain of watching your child make life-changing decisions based on a temporary emotion. I understand the passion that arises that could be misconstrued as anger when it comes to trying to prevent said decisions. I understand the disappointment. I understand the need to forgive them. I understand the guilt. I understand, I understand.

One of the most powerful lessons I learned from my mom is that God is real. And He can do anything! I was about 11 years old when my oldest brother had an accident at work. He worked in a lumber yard and was holding a stake for a co-worker, and his hand was hit with a sledgehammer. When we got the news, I watched my mom get up and go into prayer. They rushed him to the hospital, and they called my mom with the grim news that he would possibly lose his hand. There was a slim chance that if he didn't lose his hand, he would for sure lose his pointer finger and the hand would likely not be useful any longer.

My mom, without even seeing the state the hand was in for herself, told the doctor to wrap him up and send him home. I could hear the Dr. in disbelief asking her to repeat herself. He emphatically reminded her that infection could easily set in, and he could lose his whole arm, maybe even die. She calmly repeated herself, "Wrap him up, and send him home." Then she went back into her room to talk to God.

When my brother got home, totally doped up and crying, telling my mom he didn't want to lose his hand, she instructed me to come with her into the bathroom while she grabbed some medical supplies. I looked at her like, *what in the world is going on!?* I'm thinking was my mom a doctor and I didn't know? I washed my hands as she instructed and stood ready to be her assistant. As my brother sat down, I could see the fear in his eyes, but my mom was so confident, unmoved. I was in awe of her. As she unwrapped his bandages, I laid eyes on the scariest thing I had ever seen. It was like something out of a movie. Just open flesh with little white chips in it. The finger was completely unrecognizable. The bones in his hand completely shattered. The doctors literally just wrapped him up and sent him home. My brother looked and almost passed out. But my mom just acted like this was any normal activity. She prayed peace for my brother, cleaned his hand, poured blessed oil on it, and prayed. She did that every day, three times a day for the next seven days. Each day his hand was unwrapped, I expected to see another miracle. By the end of the week, what looked like a mangled piece of flesh began to resemble a finger. A few more weeks, and he regained mobility in hand. To this day, only a scar exists.

That day, I learned GOD IS REAL. And my mother knew Him, and He heard her. That day, a reverence for

God was birthed, and it set me on a course of relationship with Him I never thought I would have. I owe that to my mother. She had unwavering and unmovable faith. She taught me "If God said it, you can stake your life on it!" That kind of faith costs something. What did she have to give up, what did she have to let go to get to that place in God? While there will always be things about my mom that will remain a mystery, one thing is extremely clear. I wanted to act just like her when it came to her faith in God's ability to be God! She was the perfect picture of grace under pressure. She had a heart of pure gold. Her sacrifices and selflessness as a mother continue to bless my life even after she's gone. Being a mother is not for the faint of heart. It is the most under-appreciated institution. If you have your mother still with you, hug her, tell her you understand, forgive her, pray for her—she needs to hear it. You don't know what it cost her.

My Alysha,

I was sitting here thinking about the day you
came into my life. I was in labor for two days, and
since you were my first, I had no idea about what to
expect. I remember thinking I couldn't wait to hear
your voice. To see your smile, to smell that baby smell.
I wondered would you like me. Would you ever know
how in love I was with this little person I had never
even met? Little did I know what was in store when
this fireball entered the world. Small but fierce! In a
moment, you changed everything about who I thought
I was as a person, a woman...I was now a mother! I
was *your* mother.

You had the most electric disposition, always had
the most to say. Instantly took to music and singing.
You loved to sing. At all times, I remember peeking in
your room to see you in your bed singing and rocking
"Oh come let us adore Him." Much to the dismay
of your siblings, I might add. But you had such a
love and passion for music and people that I had
never seen. I wondered what kind of person would
you become. I knew I had my work cut out for me...
because I knew your parents ☺. But I must say I have
enjoyed the challenge.

You are almost 30! Can you believe that? And
I have to say I am so very proud of the woman you
have become. Being your mom has been one of the
greatest joys of my life. Even though sometimes it
may not have felt like it! I can't wait to see what God
has in store for you. I can't wait to one day meet my
granddaughter who I know is going to make you wish
you were nicer to me! ☺ I can't wait to see all that
you will accomplish, the lives you will touch. I am

praying that you find the peace and purpose I found in God. That you allow Him to order your steps, heal what's broken, and prove that He is who He says He is. With everything in me, I love you. I wish I could put into words what you mean to me.

I pray you BE BLESSED in your life and strive to bless someone else. BE STRONG in the Lord and the power of His might! BE FEARLESS, for there is NOTHING God can't bring you through. BE YOU 'cause everyone else is taken, and YOU are amazing.

With much love,

Mommy

My AlyiahBug!

You came into my life at such a crazy time. I was six months pregnant before I even knew you were in there. I had so many mixed emotions because of the state my life was in. I was so worried that I would bring you into a bad situation and damage your life. For the next three months, fear shaped everything I did.

When you finally arrive, you came with such a calm that I hadn't experienced with your siblings. You were so still, so reserved, and this peaceful presence that was you arrested my doubts. Little did I know that you were going to save my life! Taking care of you during all the chaos settled me. It reminded me I still had work to do. Your smile or your cry would bring me out of the prison of my own thoughts.

You always had a quiet stubbornness that challenged the way I had always dealt with issues. You were so different from your siblings that you made me go back to the drawing board and relearn some things. When I look at you now, I remember the smile that saved my life. I know you have some challenges of your own you are dealing with now. I know that I may not always have understood, or even listened. But I hope you know how dear you are to my heart. How I wouldn't even be here if it weren't for God ordaining a surprise plot twist in my story. I thank Him every day for using you to heal what was broken.

My prayer is that you find peace in Him that is unique to you. I pray you allow Him to heal your heart, regulate your mind, and stabilize your emotions. I love you more than life, Bug! I am so proud

of your strength, your determination, and your drive.
I pray that you BE BETTER than me; you have
something in you I don't, details, details, details!
BE STRONGER than me; you are definitely stronger than you think. BE BOLDER than me; never let
anything or anyone intimidate or silence your voice! I
love you, Bug!

            With all my heart,
            Mom

Lessons from My Mother

By

Alyiah D. Owens
(Jennifer C. Rogers)

Let me start by saying I am who I am because of my mother. My mom raised me to be strong and confident in who I am. She taught me to never be afraid or back down from a challenge. Keep your word and do your very best at whatever is handed to you.

She also taught me about how God's word really works. I remember when I was in elementary school, and I had to get a shot in the nurse's office. I am a person who is terrified of needles and was not having it, and I gave that nurse a run for her money. I told her if she called my brother down to the office, I would get the shot... I lied. I was just buying myself some time. She called my brother down there, and he tried to calm me down, and that didn't work. So of course, the next step was to call my mom.

I'm pretty sure when she answered the phone, she heard me screaming in the background. One thing I can say is a mother knows her child's cry. She got up to the school as fast as she could, and I was just crying and screaming. She took me out of the office and got me to calm down. Not how most people would think—by looking at my mom, some would say she is very intimidating. She sat me down and with a calm voice she told me to breathe and that everything was going to be ok. She quoted a scripture to me: "I can do all things through Christ which strengthened me" (Phil. 4:13). She made me repeat it multiple times until I actually believed it. By the time I got done repeating it, I was done crying and my breathing was steady. She looked at me and said, "Now let's do this, and if you don't, you're getting a whooping." She smiled her famous smile, and we got up and I got the shot.

My mom is my anchor. No one else can bring me back to a place of peace like her. That childhood memory stays with me always. I remind myself every day of that scripture, and I also remind myself that if nobody else is for me, my mom always is. She never wants to see me fail or in any type of pain. She is the type of mom that just wants to help and make things better.

Even to this day, she has not stopped trying to help, and I'm grown now. I guess it's true what they say, a mother's job is never done. I'm going to hold my mom to that because I still have trouble making appointments for myself. Every time I get frustrated (which is very often), she is the first person I call and vent to.

I still look to her for solutions because I know she will always have the best intentions. We may not agree on everything, but one thing we can agree on is that she

37

gives us all her very best. Growing up, my mom and I had a pretty rocky relationship. I blamed her for a lot of things; I only saw things from my side. I blamed my mom for things that she doesn't even know about, but as a kid, it made sense to me to blame her. It took me turning 21 to honestly see that my mom gave me what she had. My expectations for her as a mother were very high, and I never took into account that she was also human. She makes mistakes, and she never tried to make it seem like she was perfect.

I know now that she had to grow up with us, she had a lot going on in her life being divorced and raising three kids alone by the time she turned 25; her load was especially heavy. As a child, I would have never come to this realization because it just wouldn't have made sense; however, I'm glad that I am able to better understand that now.

Everything happens for a reason, and no matter how bad it is, I would always tell myself to stop blaming my mom even if it was something I felt like she could control. My mom would always get the worst of my frustration. I can honestly say that I am grateful for the mother I have, and I appreciate her for always giving us her very best. I want to thank her for going above and beyond as a parent even when it wasn't appreciated.

With all my heart, I love you, Mom!

Dear Momma,

First off, I want to say thank you for being my mom. You didn't have much of a choice but thank you anyway. I know things haven't always been the best between us. We've both made some mistakes, but I'm thankful that we've learned from them. I honestly appreciate you for being who you are. I admire your strength. When I think about some of the things you've been through, I just know if it were me, I wouldn't have been able to handle it. Growing up, I can remember being surprised that you didn't break under the pressure of everything you had going on. That may sound bad, but it was because I knew I was struggling. So, I expected you to struggle just like me. I never saw you break—maybe you did it in private, but you never let your kids see you weak or down. You were always like a super mom. I just want you to know that I love you, and I could not have asked for a better mom. I admire your relationship with God; I hope one day I'll be able to accomplish that. I love you, and I just want you to live the life you deserve. Through all the sacrifices you have made, you deserve the world.

Love,
Bug

I Was Listening

By
Alysha M. Owens
(Jennifer C. Rogers)

A couple of years ago, someone who barely knew me said, "You are NOTHING like your mother. She's strong. She's a fighter. She's been through a lot, and strength was her only option. You are NOT her. You're weak, pretending to be strong." This came out of nowhere! And as I stood there completely awestruck, not knowing what to say, engulfed in anger with tears rolling down my face, I remembered what my mother taught me.

My mom taught me not to let those who have never taken the time to get to know me tell me who I am. She taught me how to walk in the knowledge of who I am and who I belong to. She taught me to be myself always, even if it wasn't popular. As a teen my mother would always tell me, "Everyone isn't going to like you, baby. Everyone doesn't have good taste in people, and THAT isn't your problem!" While I listened to her, I didn't really believe that there would honestly be people that didn't like me. I mean…I'm ME, right?

I'm awesome! Man, was I wrong! About people not liking me—not about my being awesome. That's clearly true.

My mother is strong, she's a fighter, and she taught me how to be one as well. She's been through a lot in her life, so she found out early that sometimes the only thing you can do is trust God and keep going.

By the time she was 25 years old, she was divorced and a single mother of three young children. She was often exhausted, overworked, and stressed out, yet she pressed forward, always giving her children everything she had because true mothers don't make their children optional.

My siblings and I have always been my mom's first priority. She always jumps in to help us in any way she can. She'll drop everything she's doing to make sure we're okay. I remember being in elementary school, and during recess, I decided to race two of my friends. The race started, and I was in the lead! I turned my head around to gloat while still running, tripped over something, and met the concrete face first! I remember screaming at the top of my lungs, tears streaming down my face as my teacher walked me to the nurse's office. Somehow, my little brother got wind of what happened and met me at the office. The moment he walked in, he fell to his knees and cried...that's when I knew it was bad. All I could do was cry. I was hurt and helpless. They called my mom and told her what happened.

By the time she arrived, the assistant principal had gotten me to calm down; she was rubbing my back, and I began to fall asleep. My mom walked in and looked at me. Her eyes were huge as if a major freak out was coming. However, she stopped herself, took a breath, tilted her head, flashed her famous smile, and said, "Hi, baby girl." And with those two simple words, I was a puddle of tears once again. She came to my aid, held me, and told me that I was still beautiful even though I felt that I looked like a distorted monster of some sort.

My life was, and still is sometimes, full of moments like that. Moments where my mom was my safe place and protection. Moments where even though she was exhausted, she found the strength to put me first and take care of me. The strength to fight for me. To get up early in the morning and call my name out in prayer while I was sound asleep down the hall. Strength that rested in her immense love for me. She was able to go beyond her human limitations because her love for me has no limitations. She's a warrior and my personal superhero. And everything she has in her was placed in me. I am strong, and I am a fighter. Not because of who my mother is but because of the will to fight on that she placed in me. I am who I am because I was raised by the most amazing and inspiring woman. And I'm so completely blessed to call her mommy.

So, a couple of years ago when that person who barely knew me decided to come at me with "You are nothing like your mother," I decided to walk away. I didn't say a word or fight back. That didn't mean I didn't have anything to say. It just meant that I came to a resolve in myself something my mom always told me, "Just because someone says something about you doesn't make it the truth. It's up to you to decide whether you will be what they see or what God said you are."

Thank you, Mommy...I told you I was listening!

Dear Mommy,

Words could never really describe how I feel about you, but hopefully this letter does an adequate job.

In every action movie, we see the same five stages. The hero starts out fine, living their normal life. Then a villain or an imminent threat of some sort is identified. Next, they prepare to eliminate the threat in order to save lives. They go to war, and just when it begins to look like they won't win, they tap into a strength they didn't know they had and take out their adversary. I said all of that to say this: I've had the amazing honor and privilege of seeing you at every stage. I've gotten to see you at your best and watch you as you fight through things that could be deemed the worst. For this reason and so many others, I call you my personal superhero. You're a fearless warrior in every way.

I just want to thank you for teaching me to fight. To stand flat footed on what I believe regardless of who doesn't like it. To never give up no matter how hard it gets. Thank you for fighting for me even if you had to fight me in order to do it. Thank you for being extraordinarily extra at all times. And not caring who doesn't like it. Thank you for teaching me how to love myself past my insecurities and to see the true beauty in who I am always. For teaching me to never let anyone tell me who I am but to walk in the knowledge of who I am and whose I am every day of my life. Thank you for every sacrifice you made for me and my siblings in order to get us to where we are today. They are still seen and felt even in our adulthood. Thank you for always putting us first. For always having our best interest at heart and for never being afraid to say something when we weren't making the best decisions. Thank you for being our protection and our first line of defense. Thank you for being the true definition of a mother, wife, and a woman.

I could continue thanking you for everything you've done, but that would take all day. You've done *that* much for me. But I'll just sum up the rest by saying once again, THANK YOU!!! I truly hope that I'm making you proud. God knows you make me a proud daughter every day. I love you so much, Mommy, and thank you again for everything.

Love always,

Lysh

Strong Bonds Don't Break

By

Dr. LaKisha Irby

I remember when I first conceived with my husband. I dreamed of hearing angels singing as an old mentor was entering my hospital room after I had given birth. In the dream, I was holding a baby, but I didn't know the sex of the child. I was miserably married, but I was still a wife when I conceived. The mature know what I mean. The only book I read during my pregnancy was Prayers and Promises for Supernatural Childbirth by Jackie Mize. The day my daughter entered this world, the only prayer I prayed was for God to make me a good mother. You see, while in my marriage, I was told by my then-husband that I was unable to take care of myself so how would I be able to care for our daughter. I was disrespected, cursed out, threatened to be put out, and I was emotionally and financially abused throughout the duration of my marriage. One thing I knew for sure was that I was not going to bring my child into this world to see her mother being treated and talked to like a dog.

Along with an abusive husband, I know what it's like to have a damaged relationship with my mother. My mother is the type of woman who if you disagree with her, or if she doesn't get her way with you, she will begin to try to manipulate you through slander, manipulation, and planting seeds of discord. This is another example of a type of toxic relationship, and I've had to learn over the years to protect myself and my daughter. Even having a relationship with my father has been strained in a sense due to the toxicity of my mother.

I'm a firm believer that through marriage you become one. My relationship with my father had to have some distance as well because of my mother. Within the last few months, family counseling has taken place, and my father and the counselor had to get my mother to understand that what she continues to do and has done in the past is wrong. Her behavior has improved somewhat, but when you have done wrong for so long, that behavior becomes a habit. I do believe it was through my uncle and my grandmother having a firm talk with my father on several occasions in getting him to understand that if he didn't stand up to be the man and leader of his household and to stand for truth, he was going to lose his relationship with his daughter. I don't allow my mother to keep my daughter for long periods of time because of her mental state and what I know she has done to me over the years. This is not being done in a spiteful manner, but to protect the mental and emotional state of an innocent child.

Fast forward eight years later, Dreamer, my daughter shared a dream with me. In her conversation, she said, "God taught me how to drive, so I can drive!" As her mother, I knew that dream meant I needed to tighten the reins. In Dreamer's mind, she was the boss of me instead of me being a mother and the disciplinarian that leads her in the right direction in life. As Dreamer's mother, I know she is an anointed child, so she has to be disciplined not only in life but also to hear the voice of God for herself and to deliver messages to others.

A lot of what I have gone through and experienced in my childhood with my own mother has influenced and shaped how I relate to my daughter. I don't want to be known as the mother who didn't put the time into cultivating that relationship. My daughter is fortunate enough to be homeschooled and is with me throughout the day while I operate multiple businesses, so she is getting the best of both worlds. She is still quite active with extracurricular activities that include lessons in music, computer, swimming, dance, and Girl Scouts.

I know my relationship with her is imperative. I have had to fight to keep her in my custody due to a still bitter ex-husband who is upset that I left his abusive behavior when I was pregnant with our daughter. I lived in Flowery Branch, Georgia, during the duration of our short marriage, but exactly one year later, moved back to South Carolina to escape his consistent abuse. His abusive rants were emotional and financial in nature, not to the point where it was physical, but I do believe it was headed there. It was a form of control that included what I could purchase from the grocery store to eat. I was told if I got fat, he would leave me even though I was a housewife who depended on him financially a few months into our marriage, finding out I was pregnant after I was planning to leave. It was a tumultuous marriage, but there was a beautiful baby girl that was produced out of it. I always say I have the best part of my ex-husband, and that is our daughter.

There is a direct correlation between your upbringing and how your relationships with others are formed. That strong mother-daughter relationship is what I desired for my mother and me, so that's why I pour so much into Dreamer. Dreamer will say when she doesn't get her way that she wants to go to live with her daddy because he is nicer. As her mother, I don't take those words or insults personally because I know it's coming from a place of the immaturity of an 8-year-old and also from a place where there is limited structure in Daddy's home when she visits. As her mother, but as a woman first, I know the importance of education and making your own way. Even if her decision is to become a housewife, it's imperative that she understands financial literacy.

An able body should never leave their livelihood in the hands of someone else. I was listening to a mentor that shared a story about a woman who was also a housewife, but experienced life the hard way. This woman was in her sixties, was married to an attorney who left her for another woman and left her with nothing. He was able to maneuver through the system and his relationships in the system to leave her without. I'm pouring into my daughter what a traditional education could never offer. She's protective of me as her mother, just as I am with her. It is my duty to guide her and mold her into the empowered woman she will later become.

*My name is **Dreamer LaRice Irby**, and I have the sweetest mommy ever. My mommy is my best friend. I love her so much. Sometimes, she can be mean, but I know I love her. We go to the mall together, we work together, and we sleep together. My mommy cares for me, and I'm glad she bought me a new dog named Brownie. My mommy is great to me. My mommy makes me want to kiss her 100 hundred times. My mommy and I have a great relationship because we have a great family. When I say I want to go to live with my daddy, it's because my mommy is mean sometimes. My mommy disciplines me when I am disobedient and when I don't do all of my work. I know my mommy doesn't want me to be disobedient because I don't want to disappoint Jesus and God or myself. I love Jesus and God, and I know I respect them.*

Dreamer loves to travel, eat well, and stay in nice hotels. She loves to see me get dressed for my speaking engagements and functions. Matter of fact, she insists on being there. God is showing her who and what she is going to do when she comes of age, even before me. My assignment is to pour into her so her calling will exceed and be greater than mine. She won't be persuaded by a no-good man because she will be used to the finer things in life. Mediocre won't do. Mistreatment won't do. Disrespect and dishonor won't do. My relationship with Dreamer is based on the fact that I asked God the day she was born to make me a good mother. We have a bond. A bond I pray will not ever be broken by her growth or age.

I want her to feel as if she can always come to me about anything, no matter how painful it may be. If I can't answer her questions, then I will find someone who can. What I have learned as a mother is not to become offended by what a child says out of anger because it's an offense. It's not them; it's being said out of an emotion, not facts. I've also learned to pay attention to her behavior in a spiritual sense, not just what I see in the natural. An outsider, such as my mother or a complete stranger, may say I need to discipline my daughter more physically as in spanking, but I know as her mother to always take into account what's going on spiritually before I address her physically.

What works for one child may not work for another. Spanking a child may work in one situation or not allowing a child to watch a certain program on television that's influencing that behavior, may be the solution. A spanking isn't a solution without a lesson following. The same way we had to learn as a child that had to grow into a woman, give your daughter room to make mistakes, but also give the guidance for them to learn lessons and grow from them. Dreamer knows how to apologize when she is wrong, even at her young age. That is powerful in itself because she's not allowing her pride to get the best of her. I've had to apologize to her as her mother as well. That skill alone will take her far in many relationships rather it be romantic, friendships, or associations.

On this journey, many times we may have to be the

bigger person. Many of the decisions I have made professionally and personally is because of my most precious gift from God. It's a gift to be a mother. God has blessed me in the overflow in that area by blessing me with an early childcare facility where I am a mother figure to other children. I'm a Girl Scout troop leader and have poured into other children. I do remember when my ex-husband spoke the words that I was not going to be a good mother to someone else because I was unable to care for myself, but the big God I serve proved otherwise. One thing about Dreamer is that she will speak the truth. One thing I see in the Body of Christ is the need for the women of wisdom to step into their rightful steed to mother the new mothers and teach the younger generation how to become and prepare themselves to become a wife.

Women of today know what it means to be a Proverbs 31 woman in a business sense, but we need to know fully what it means to walk in a spirit of excellence as a woman and a wife. I do believe in the power of the bond between a mother and her daughter, and it is a bond if properly tended to and cared for that can't easily be broken.

Dear Dreamer,

I pray that all of your days are filled with joy, love, and peace beyond understanding. As my daughter, you have brought nothing but pure joy to my life. I know every day isn't going to be easy, but one thing I know without a shadow of doubt is that I serve a God who will teach you how to dance in the rain. You have nothing short of greatness in you, and I expect you to operate with a spirit of excellence in all of your endeavors. Know that every sacrifice I've made was a decision with you in mind. Every enemy I've fought for you didn't stand a chance, and it would be a cold day in hell if they thought they would win the fight against me. You are special, you are anointed, you are prosperous, and you're going to be everything God has called you to be. You are a Proverbs 31 woman in training that only a true faithful and loyal man of God will be able to see. You are blessed in your coming and your going. Your children call you blessed, your husband call you blessed, and praise you. Never doubt who you are because God has called you and chose you. Many are called, but few are chosen. Babygirl, you are chosen, so walk with your head held high because you represent the King who sits on high. Work hard but play even harder. Take the time to enjoy life. Travel and see the world, even if you have to go at it alone. Live life to the fullest because you only get one. I leave you with this, your mother's legs and shoulders are strong, but God is going to make yours even stronger. I speak blessings over you, my beautiful baby girl.

Love,

Your Mommy

The Blessing of a Mother

By

LaTasha S. Thompson

A woman of strength, courage, and grace. The epitome of what women strive to be. The Proverbs 31 woman, whose virtue is worth more than rubies. Deborah A. Thompson is my Proverbs 31 woman. The first bond in life is between a child and their mother. That bond can either be nurtured or abandoned. Thank be to God, I was blessed with a mother who chose to nurture and cultivate our relationship.

I was born the eldest of three—and the only girl. Our parents raised us with Christian standards and morals. My mother was "First Lady," and the way she carried herself and how she raised her family were always under constant scrutiny and evaluation. Her small stature did not stop her from making her mark in this world. A woman of many talents and many virtues. Yeah, a void was left when Deborah exchanged this world for another, but let's start from the beginning.

As a child, all I remember is my mother being there. She was there for our family, of course, but she was also there for everybody else. She was someone who believed in keep it real. Sugar coating things wasn't her style; straight with no chaser is how she was. Growing up, she was my She-Ro—she could do it all. Helping with my art projects, hemming my brother's pants, and cooking all in the same moment. Momma came from a musical family, so she ensured that we were musical, too. I would often wonder why my classmates would call my mother "Mama" or make such statements like, "Ask if I can spend the night" or "I wish I was your sister." It wasn't until later that I realized those classmates were missing something in their own mother/daughter relationship. What I had was priceless, and little did I know how priceless it was. In my younger years, I would get upset because I thought my friends' mothers were cooler. Truth be told, I had a pretty cool mom. It just appeared that my friends had more of a friendship type of relationship and not one as strict as my own mother/daughter relationship. I remember being chastised for something and expressing to her that I wanted to be able to talk to her like she was my friend. Mama yelled, "I am not your friend!"

The hurt feelings I had were indescribable. Why didn't my mama want to be my friend, I thought. We, rather I, got a quick understanding. She made sure I understood I would respect her as my mother not her home girl. I can remember the Saturday nights she would make us prepare for church...that was a struggle. I was all for hot bubble baths and ironing whatever needed to be; however, her rule was if you want any type of curl in your hair the next morning you better put rollers in it (yup, she was old school). Now, here I was in the '90s; all we ever did was curl and flatiron our hair. There were so many bad hair days from those ugly sponge rollers. I laugh now and think, "Oh, the struggle." Guess who put rollers in their hair this very day? Yup, this girl.

Like most children, I couldn't wait to leave home to feel independent and spread my wings. It didn't matter because I called home three to four times a day. Returning home, I noticed that my mama had loosened the parental reins. It wasn't that I was "acting up" but growing up. To be honest, I wasn't acting wild like you would think. Remember, I come from a long line of ministers, pastors, and preachers, so image was everything. It wasn't just about image, however, but her teaching me how to live by the Word of God to where He would be pleased. At the end of the day, it wasn't so much about what others thought but what God knew. By the way, we preachers' kids are not necessarily the worst.

Be real, at some point you thought it, but it's ok. Imagine being almost 40 and still hearing that same cliché. As a young adult, I saw Momma in a different light. I watched my mother be a true "help mate" to my father and his ministry. Many nights, I knew she wanted him on time for dinner or just be home but because of the calling of church business, it sometimes took him away. She made sure home was taken care of and we children needed nothing. When it came to Dad's ministry, she felt the need to start a ministry of her own. So, she began to mentor women younger than she, particularly younger women understand what this life was about. No matter your past, no matter what's currently going on in this life, there is a life beyond this one. If you live right here on earth, there are rewards in the life to come. She had a really close friend that had been diagnosed with pancreatic cancer. She would go wherever she was to minister and encourage her. They often would talk about what heaven was like.

Momma and I often talked hypothetically about our final moments, but this time was reality. Momma had gotten severely ill in 2007, and God allowed her to recover and come home. In 2008, she became ill just like in 2007—almost to the day. This time, just like that, my momma was gone. We were preparing for our momma's friend to pass away; we didn't think we would see the day when Momma left this world first. Talk about a shocker. When I look back, 2007 was an indication of what was coming; we just didn't know it. Reflecting back, I do know that God allowed the time between the first and second illness events. Please believe our family and the church showered her with love and appreciation to let her know what she truly meant to us before her passing. So, when she passed, it was a hard pill to swallow nationwide.

The most conflicting time in my life is when I heard the nurse say, "I'm sorry for your loss." What was life going to be like without my mama? She had been here to help everybody. Who was going to help me? To this very day, I hate Mother's Day. It's only a reminder of what I don't have, and it seems to be pushed in my face, especially since it is so commercialized. I will say the sting of it all isn't as bad. Being raised in the church and my family working in the funeral business, we knew we weren't on this earth to stay. We definitely were not immune to death, but we just didn't expect to it so soon. Losing my mom at twenty-five had me feeling emotions I couldn't convey. The blessing in losing her at twenty-five is knowing that I've had my mom longer than some. What I did know was there was a major life adjustment that needed to be made, and I needed God's help to do it. I never stop praying for my family, asking God to give us peace, comfort, and wisdom. I constantly prayed for my dad, my brothers and prayed even harder for my grandmother as my mom was the third child she had to bury. I also prayed for my church family as they had lost their First Lady.

God had answered my prayers of peace and comfort in moments I needed it most because when I look back, I thought this life would be too hard to live without her. BUT GOD! Just when you think life is unlivable, He always makes a way to let the sun shine through the darkness. People always say it gets easier, but I'm not sure about that. What I do know is I've learned to adjust. With each life's milestone, the sadness and void are ever present. To know that she will not attend my wedding or help me with future children is sad and disheartening. At the end of the day, I have to keep living. There are even moments where I still call her number, just to realize she won't answer. You would think that thirteen years later, I would be used to not calling her or saying her name, but I still have my moments. I've also learned having "moments" is ok; in fact, it's normal.

In the present day, those that have lost their mothers ask me how I do it. I tell them I have adjusted but not by my own strength but those who have experienced the same thing and the strength God has given me. In the moment, there is a sense of confusion and being lost, but there were women who made sure I was ok, mentally, physically, and spiritually, and that mattered. Shortly after burying my mom, I became critically ill, and I needed her the most. I thank God that my dad was there and still is there; however, it's nothing like a mother's love and care. I prayed and never lost my trust in what God's will is.

Growing up listening to my father preach many eulogies, he would always say, "You hear the deceased more in death than in life." I promise you he's right. There are times I can hear her "two cents" about a situation. For instance, *never forget who you are and where you come from. Always be and act like a lady.* I can definitely hear her tell me to make sure that God is pleased with everything I did in life. In those moments, I smile because it shows me that I'll never forget the lessons she taught me, and her voice has become part of my conscience. Her influence will never abandon me.

As I an adult, I saw my mother for the selfless woman she was. In turn, I made sure she knew if nobody else appreciated her, I did. There were times I would slip money into her hand and wallet for her to spend on herself, but she would take that and use it on others. So, I started taking her to the mall, nail shop and hair salon with me to pamper her. She was so deserving of it. Those were our times to bond and get close. While my mother looked out for others, I made sure I looked out for her. The least I could have done was make sure life for her was pleasant as much as I could.

Like most mother/daughter relationships, ours wasn't always perfect; however, there was never a moment that we didn't love, trust, and have each other's back. I see mothers and daughters who argue and fight like strangers in the street, and that's when I miss my mom most. I get so frustrated watching something so disrespectful and disturbing. I wish my momma was here, and this is how you treat the woman who gave you life? You're a foolish woman, I say! There will be a day when you must part ways, not by choice but by the Will of the Lord. Any relationship that is left unresolved stays that way. So, if you need to make a phone call, write a letter, send a text, do that. I would give anything to hear my mother say my name, cook a meal, or simply just be there one last time.

What I've learned in the passing of my mother is that life goes on. Time doesn't stand or wait for anybody. I would joke about how my mood would change from minute to minute, but I was trying to adjust. Adjusting becomes your norm. In conversation, I tell people not to let others dictate how you grieve. As long as it's healthy and safe, do what helps you. By all means, find something positive, productive, and therapeutic to help you adjust. Some need to scream, others need to keep busy, and some write.

Believe me when I tell you it all helps.

Though I felt cheated, stunned, and perplexed, I realized that in the twenty-five years I had her with me, she equipped me with all that I needed to keep going. She taught me that in times of confusion, darkness, and uncertainty I need to lean on my faith, pray before making any life decision, and not to beat myself up if I fall short. Keep trying. Stand up for what's right even if that means standing alone. If my mother was here today, I would hope that she would be proud of us. If she could see us, I would hope that she's proud in how we've adjusted and her life, influence, and lessons taught were not in vain.

To My First Lady,

February 5, 2008, was life changing to say the least. I never thought I would lose you so soon. As times goes on, I find myself readjusting to the fact you're no longer here. What I do know is your influence is very present. It's amazing how after all this time, people still speak of what you did for them and how much they miss and love you. It's been said that you were the most down to earth and realest of them all. I couldn't agree more.

As I look at the family, I could only hope that you would be proud of us. We have all had our personal storms at one moment or another, but we have kept God first and stuck together has a family. Believe it or not, I don't make major decisions without you in mind. For the twenty-five years that I had you, you instilled and taught me so much. I thank you for being who you were in this life.

Although I know you are resting peacefully in the bosom of the Creator, I wish you could be here for life's milestones. On February 23, 2020, I got engaged to a wonderful man. What's funny is I know you would approve and love him. Knowing that makes my heart smile. I truly hope you knew how much you are loved. Life is so different without you, but we keep pushing forward as you would have it.

I never said goodbye because I will see you again, so I'll say...UNTIL NEXT TIME!

Forever in my heart,
LaTasha Sherree'

Girl Interrupted

By
Kimberly Cox

The funeral was over, the phone calls of support had stopped, and all of the food had been eaten. It was now time for me to come out of my cocoon, my insulated, protected place and face the harsh reality. I awoke early this particular morning, physically moving about but emotionally fatigued. I remember going into the bathroom purposely avoiding the mirror because I didn't want to see. Unfortunately, I caught a glimpse, then I looked, and that look grew into a stare. I leaned in closely, examining this encrypted, motherless version of myself and said, "I'm different now, and everybody knows it." I was a 13-year-old girl transitioning into a new world, processing death for the very first time. Just barely two weeks ago, I had unexpectedly severed ties with my mom, the woman who gave life to me, unconditionally loved me and, with great devotion, taught me. Despite the issues that plagued her, which at times made our family seem dysfunctional, I could not fathom a world where she would not exist, yet I was suddenly there having to wrangle my thoughts and return to school. I had heard the older adults interject in their conversations with my dad, "You better watch them, they (my 16-year-old sister and I) are hurt and afraid, and they may act out in all kinds of ways." I knew that aside from the pain and fear that they so candidly spoke of, I also felt an unmerciful weight of embarrassment and shame. You see this was an era when the family unit or nucleus was more traditional, and mine as I knew it, mom, dad, sisters and brother no longer existed, and I didn't know how to be, but most importantly how I would be perceived because I was different.

I was somewhat discombobulated by the time I made it to school. I was fumbling around in my locker when I felt someone in my space tap me on the shoulder. It was one of the very handsome, junior-varsity star basketball players. He bent down and said, "I'm sorry about your mom," then he kissed me, squarely on the lips. Oddly enough, that kiss played a significant role in comforting my teenage soul. It was that sweet, affectionate gesture that gave me permission to release those feelings of angst and welcomed me back. Unfortunately, it didn't spark any romance, but it definitely lowered my anxiety. In retrospect, God often uses unconventional ways and unlikely sources to heal, strengthen, and comfort us. He knew that fried chicken and chocolate cake wouldn't work this time, so he used one of my peers, the popular jock, to be the soothing balm that I so desperately needed.

My sister and I had to mature quickly. We took over the domestic duties such as meal planning, grocery shopping, cooking daily meals, cleaning, and we even handled paying the monthly bills. There was no online guide like Pinterest nor was there an adult relative giving advice or checking in us. We were completely on our own and trying to emulate our mother. However, we felt an insurmountable amount of pressure, and many days we were afraid as we were getting accumulated into this new role. For example, our dad would take us to the grocery store, give us money, and sit in the car. The amount of money would vary from week to week, so we would take a calculator and a list to secure food, cleaning supplies, and personal toiletries. Sometimes, there would be a ruckus in the store because of our disagreement on which items to remove from the basket and which ones to keep, but we were figuring it out. Being raised through the lens of a masculine perspective presented its own set of challenges. I was a very affectionate child who looked for him to return the favor, but oftentimes would get a strange look or scoffed at. I believe I was sixteen, and I asked him, "Dad, do you love me?" he replied, "The lights are on, you have a roof over your head, and food, right?" That is how he equated love, through provision. My dad's masculine nurturing and affection were demonstrated through three basic concerns at this point: a roof over your head (not a lavish fuchsia pink and purple bedroom), food (beans, greens, and cornbread not McDonald's), and clothes on your back (not trend-setting clothes). I used to show my dad cute outfits from the sale circulars in the newspaper, begging for clothing allowances, but was unsuccessful most of the time. He was a practical man, so all of the extra items that a teen would consider a necessity (like lip gloss, sunglasses, and purses) often got shot down. This became a family mantra, but for me, it was a real struggle. I was frustrated, I felt I needed an advocate, so God in his infinite wisdom, sent one.

I spent the next year or so engaged at church. I often tell people the black church will teach you everything you need to know about life—the good, bad, and ugly. One of my bad and ugly experiences came on Mother's Day. Historically, I believe we can all agree that Mother's Day Holiday is held in very high esteem, especially in the black church. They go all out to showcase the role of the mother in the family unit, their hard labor and beautiful sacrifices.

Mothers and their children show up to Sunday service immaculately dressed with matching hats, neckties, shoes, purses, and the like. Sometimes, there were pageants, speeches, and poems, all odes to sweet mom. Some of them adorned their outfits with fresh rose corsages, red if your mother was living and white if she was deceased. This particular year, they wanted to make sure ALL of the children in the church wore a rose. I was in a precarious situation, so I decided to bypass the line to the fellowship hall and go into the sanctuary. One of the efficient (and I say that sarcastically) church mothers spotted me and handed me a red rose and said, "Put this on, chile." Meanwhile, another one looked over at me and said, "Oh no, she gets a white one." Well, I saw those two ladies rush and scramble around until they found one of the older church mothers and convinced her to give me her white corsage so that I could be correctly represented on this Mother's Day. There I was, fourteen years old, standing amidst the children of the church, who were all wearing red rose corsages or boutonnieres with my white one. In my very youthful mind, that act symbolized, reinforced, and reminded me that I was different. I was hoping for a route to escape, or at least an invisible cloak to hide under, but then God sent her, my fairy godmother, my advocate who said, "Take that off of her, give her a red rose. She has a mother...she has a whole church full of mothers." That affirmation and validation laid the foundation that allowed me to evolve.

I found my village, my mom-squad, or they found me.

I was in my thirties before I could sense a direct correlation between the divine providence of God and the loss of my mother as a recurring theme in my life. Through that one traumatic experience, I learned to navigate some of the toughest and most trying times in my life. Just as God used that experience to mature me mentally and emotionally, He also used it to draw me to him. I had thought many times, particularly when I was faced with pain like infertility, or confronting relational struggles, I would remember having to bear that pain but also the spiritual comfort and healing God brought. The day my mother died, it was a cold, rainy morning, but it was the running against the hardwood floors that played over and over in my mind. I heard my mother running across our living room toward the front door, and then she collapsed. The symbolism of her leaving us and this earth manifested in that moment both physically and spiritually. That is when my dad, oldest sister, and I jumped up and ran to her. I was in charge of calling the ambulance while my dad and sister attended to my mom. They were looking for physical signs of injury, then I came back, standing over them, watching for any sign of life, but there was none. Finally, the paramedics arrived and worked on her, and my middle sister and I stood in the hallway and watched as they shook their heads and told my father she was gone, but the truth is through her rich legacy, she still lives. "Yet God has made everything beautiful for its own time. He has planted eternity in the human heart, but even so, people cannot see the whole scope of God's work from beginning to end" (Ecclesiastes 3:11).

My Dear Tecumseh,

Today, I see you in all of your splendor. Your full humanity is revealed, and you are a wonder to me. Your robe is a golden reflection of your refinement. All of the disappointments, marital hardships, family hurt, and personal pain you experienced has brought us, you and I, to this point in my life. First of all, I am thoroughly impressed and godly proud of how you managed to be a stay-at-home mom to four children, endure a tumultuous marriage while wrestling with your mental illness. As a kid, I didn't understand this mystery illness, how some days we could talk and play, and others you were disengaged and angry. You would snap and lash out, but none of us were equipped to help you handle it. So, we selfishly and ashamedly distanced ourselves and left you all alone. There was no treatment plan or medicine then to relieve the pain you were experiencing, but you, my dear, somehow managed to impart incredible life lessons and resources to all of your children. You were the most ingenious and resourceful woman that I know. I marvel as I remember watching you take one chicken and one bag of rice and create a week full of meals including one of my favorite desserts, rice pudding. I am still wondering how you made that mouth-watering, cast-iron skillet cake! I realized my creative side and sense of flair came from you. You never had the opportunity to follow your dreams, but I followed one of them and became a hairstylist for eleven years.

You majorly struggled in your relationship with Daddy, but you chose a good man that cared. He had a big heart of gold, he was firm yet gentle, compassionate, and I believe, like you, he did his best. He stuck to the basics, taught us absolute self-sufficiency and allowed us to live. Of course, there were times that he was confused and made mistakes like any parent, but he took really good care of us, and in return, we took care of him. One of my fondest memories was when he walked me down the aisle, and we honored you, too. Bay stood in for you to light the unity candle. I suppose you wonder why I addressed you as Tecumseh, your name and not Mama, the name I called you. To me, you have borne many names other than Mama. I understand now, your 55-year-old adult daughter still finds herself longing for your wisdom as a woman, friend, and mentor. But the cold, hard truth is that I will never experience that with you. I will never experience quite a few things like brunch (I LOVE a good brunch), Sunday drives (they are SO relaxing), and shopping (I LOVE a great sale, definitely a nod to you). So, when I see estranged mother/daughter relationships or hear daughters disrespect their mothers or wish harm upon them, I am deeply heartbroken. I wish they could understand that mom is a woman that hurts, makes mistakes, and could use some encouragement and compassion. It has taken forty-two years, but I see you, Tecumseh.

"Go," she whispered. "Go. Show them you spell
your name W-O-M-A-N."
— Maya Angelou

Cheria Hollowell-Rush

Cheria Hollowell-Rush was born in Memphis, Tennessee; raised in Brooklyn Park, Minnesota; and resides in Menomonee Falls, WI. She is a woman of God, wife, author, a mother to her bonus son and a mother to be. She is the middle child and only girl with two brothers. Cheria is a senior technical project manager with ten years in her field. She spent two years at Xavier University in New Orleans, LA, and holds a bachelor's in business administration with a minor in human resources from Cardinal Stritch University. Cheria's love for God and passion/love for others has given her the ability to go to war in prayer for those in need. She is a prayer warrior.

Her passions are planning events, making hair products, and tapping into her creative side.

Melanie D. Phillips

Melanie D. Phillips is an entrepreneur, author, visionary, transformational speaker, certified relationship and business coach, and the CEO of Destiny Discovered Publishing. She's a woman of faith who has a double bachelor's in business administration and business management. In addition, she holds an MBA. Phillips endured a disturbing death that would ultimately change her life forever. The death of a marriage in 2016. Phillips began writing in 2016 while amidst this devastating storm, and when God spoke, she listened.

It took Phillips to go through the death of a marriage for the scales to fall off her eyes, and to her surprise, God impregnated her with a series of books: *The Mouth of Babes*. Also, she holds yearly luncheons and conferences called Strengthen the Bond. Strengthen the Bond deals with mothers and daughters whose relationships are strained, broken, and/or need improving.

Phillips is an inspirational writer that focuses on families, especially the youth. She also resides in Menomonee Falls, Wisconsin.

Learn more at WWW.MelanieDPhillips.com

LaTambria Johnson

Mariah Ross

Amaiyah Ross

A native of Dallas, Texas, LaTambria Johnson is an accomplished businesswoman who's the owner of Tam's Sweet Treats & More, a professionally operated baking business she established in 2014, which has been featured in the North Dallas Gazette and Making Headline News. Also, Johnson is a state board registered dental assistant and three-time published author. A graduate of Dallas Skyline High School, Johnson has two daughters: Amaiyah Ross, 13, and Mariah Ross, 12, and is married to longtime NBA reporter Andre Johnson.

An all-around gifted student, **Amaiyah** is a member of the National Honor Society.

Mariah also is a gifted honor student who has maintained amazing growth after being born a preemie at one pound, six ounces.

Both girls, to their credit, have launched businesses during the pandemic: Amaiyah's Art Madness and Mariah's Tye Dye.

Alysha M. Owens, Jennifer C. Rogers & Alyiah Dominique Owens

Jennifer C. Rogers

To see her now, you would never have known that Jennifer C. Rogers was just a girl who grew up with low self-esteem and low self-worth issues. You wouldn't know the amount of pain that actually hid at one time behind that smile. You would be surprised at the challenges she had to overcome, that were ultimately designed to crush her heart and destroy her spirit. But for the love and the healing power of God... She doesn't look like what she's been through!

Today, Jennifer is a minister at the Turning Point Family Worship Center, where she and her husband Wayne have head up the Locked 4 Life Marriage Ministry for the last 15 years. Jennifer has a passion for bringing the Word of God to life with couples young and old and help them make God relevant in their lives today! She believes in God's design for marriage and fights for the preservation of the family unit.

Jennifer is a dynamic speaker and workshop instructor whose animated and no-nonsense style can captivate any audience. You can feel her passion for God's people through her words and see the passion through her willingness to sacrifice for the betterment of the family, church, and community. She has been a host of several radio broadcasts, but the study of human behavior has always fascinated Jennifer. She believes if people had a deeper understanding of themselves and why they do what they do, it would go a long way in building long-lasting relationships.

Jennifer has been saved for 30 years and has a love for God that is contagious. She is married to a wonderful companion Wayne, who is also a minister and dynamite teacher in his own right. She also has three children, Alysha (26), Avery (25), and Alyiah (22). Jennifer enjoys hobbies such as decorating and event planning, and these days as an empty nester, she spends time with her newest editions, Yorkies Grace and Chase.

Alyiah Dominique Owens was born on November 28, 1998 in Indianapolis, IN. As the youngest of three children, Alyiah was often quiet and reserved. However, after middle school, she found her own voice and hasn't been afraid to use it since. She dances to the beat of her own drum and is authentically herself, always.

Alyiah has a love for teaching and working with children. She spent her early employment years putting shaping the young minds at Turning Point Schools. She is currently working as a claims adjuster for an insurance company. Alyiah has a sincere love for dogs. With her sidekick Peaches in tow, they are unstoppable. She also is an avid reader and researcher. She always does her research!

Alyiah D. Owens is original, confident, independent, passionate, a force to be reckoned with and truly so much more. She is truly destined to do great things!

Alysha M. Owens was born on November 12, 1994, and she is the first born of her mother's children. As the oldest of three, she made her mark on the family as the "Great Debater" as she started talking at 11 months and has never stopped. Always ready for a debate on just about anything!

As an avid reader and researcher, her love for new information is infectious. Her real passion is music; from a very young age, she would sing herself to sleep with songs learned in choir rehearsal and always had to have music playing even as a baby.

Alysha has a work ethic that is second to none and has interpersonal skills out of this world that enable her to form relationships very quickly. She's always ready to jump in any project and is an asset to any team.

Alysha is an anointed praise and worship leader and ordained minister at her church. She has directed a children's choir and children's praise team as well. Music is in her blood. Her passion for God and his Word is also apparent. She loves people, has never met a stranger, and isn't afraid to share the good news of the gospel with any she encounters.

Dr. LaKisha & Dreamer LaRice Irby

Dr. LaKisha Irby is a mother, mentor, serial entrepreneur, author, and a certified life and business coach. Dr. Irby finds extreme gratitude in helping others obtain their highest personal and professional level of success through joy, happiness, and dedication all through the power of choice. She enjoys inspiring others to live the life of their dreams by building confidence through empowerment. She believes that the power in positive choices create a lifestyle that will not only benefit the individual, but also the world and those around them. By serving through her community on both the local and national levels, Dr. Irby combines her professional gifts with her love for service. Her motto is that of a true Proverbs 31 woman knowing greater is He who is in me, than He that is in the world. Her daughter Dreamer LaRice Irby is a talented 8-year-old with a love for life. Dreamer loves dancing, playing the piano, singing, and playing with her favorite Shih-Poo, Brownie. The second grader is wise beyond her years and brings joy wherever she goes. One thing is for sure, her future is awaiting her, and it sure is bright!

LaTasha S. Thompson

LaTasha S. Thompson is the eldest and only girl with two brothers; she was born in Youngstown, OH, in December of 1982. In 1984, her father accepted a fulltime evangelistic position, so they moved to Milwaukee, WI, and Milwaukee has been home ever since. She graduated from Harold Vincent High and is an alumnus of Southwestern Christian College, a historical black college located in Terrell, TX. LaTasha has also studied at Cardinal Stritch University. Her goal in life has always been to help others. Assisting individuals in obtaining and maintaining employment became what she enjoyed rather than it only being just a job. Later, she wanted to continue in her purpose of helping others, so she focused on families and children working at a social service agency that focused on the well-being of underprivileged youth. Through networking, collaborating, and working in Human Resources and Social Services, she has been able to build great relationships that will last a lifetime.

In her spare time, she loves reading and writing and spending time with family. LaTasha comes from a close-knit family, and to them, family is everything. She volunteers at the church where her father has pastored for over 30 years. Although LaTasha's mom is deceased, she carries her mother's life lessons with her daily. She thanks God for the foundation that her parents laid. Her praise and faith in God have kept her through many obstacles in life. Her mantra is "I can do all things through Christ which strengthens me."

Kimberly Cox

Kimberly has been in public service for approximately 25 years. She is employed by Tennessee's legislative branch in the Office of the Chief Clerk of the House of Representatives. She received a bachelor's degree in public relations and a minor in women's studies from Middle Tennessee State University, Murfreesboro, TN; and a master's degree in organizational leadership at Trevecca Nazarene University in Nashville, TN. Because her passion is empowering women and young girls, she has the opportunity to serve in many capacities. Currently, she is the third Vice President of Membership and Scholarship Chair of the National Coalition of 100 Black Women Metro/Nashville. She is also serving as an administrator in the Daughters of the Promise, Inc., a nonprofit women's ministry dedicated to help women leaders grow in their relationship with God. In addition,

Kimberly participates with a yearly fundraiser luncheon at the Nashville Rescue Mission assisting women who are struggling with homelessness and substance abuse. One of her favorite scriptures, "To whom much is given, much will be required" (Luke 12:48) undergirds her love for people and community service. She believes that if we have been blessed with talents, wealth, knowledge, and the like, it is our responsibility to grace others. As a music and culinary enthusiast, Kimberly enjoys listening to live music, going to concerts and food festivals, and welcomes any traveling opportunity to explore and expand her palette. She also has maintained her interest in cosmetology and the beauty industry and enjoys consulting in event planning and crafting. Kimberly is a native of Memphis, TN, but currently resides in Nashville, TN with her husband Marvin, and enjoys spending time with loved ones.

A Mother-Daughter Bond

Mothers and daughters, they have a special bond.

Sometimes, they may not always agree, but it always come back to that one. That one bond that keeps them and holds them together.

The love they have for each other will last forever.

Sometimes, it is difficult, and sometimes, it is hard. Regardless of the situation, there's nothing too hard for God. God will get you through any circumstance or any trial you may go through with your mother. He will heal your brokenness and put you back on track like none other. Even if you've been adopted or been raised by another, there's still something that connects you together...that bond...that special bond of a daughter and a mother.

By: Melanie D. Phillips